Copyright © 2011 XAMonline, Inc.

All rights reserved. No part of the material protected by this copyright notice may be reproduced or utilized in any form or by any means, electronic or mechanical, including photocopying, recording or by any information storage and retrievable system, without written permission from the copyright holder.

To obtain permission(s) to use the material from this work for any purpose including workshops or seminars, please submit a written request to:

XAMonline, Inc.
25 First Street, Suite 106
Cambridge, MA 02141
Toll Free: 1-800-509-4128
Email: info@xamonline.com
Web: www.xamonline.com
Fax: 1-617-583-5552

Library of Congress Cataloging-in-Publication Data

Wynne, Sharon A.
    ILTS Assessment of Professional Teaching Tests 101-104 Practice Test 1:
    Teacher Certification / Sharon A. Wynne. -1st ed.
    ISBN: 978-1-60787-197-2
    1. ILTS Assessment of Professional Teaching Tests 101-104 Practice Test 1
    2. Study Guides   3. ILTS   4. Teachers' Certification & Licensure
    5. Careers

Disclaimer:

The opinions expressed in this publication are the sole works of XAMonline and were created independently from the National Education Association, Educational Testing Service, or any State Department of Education, National Evaluation Systems or other testing affiliates.

Between the time of publication and printing, state specific standards as well as testing formats and website information may change that is not included in part or in whole within this product. Sample test questions are developed by XAMonline and reflect similar content as on real tests; however, they are not former tests. XAMonline assembles content that aligns with state standards but makes no claims nor guarantees teacher candidates a passing score. Numerical scores are determined by testing companies such as NES or ETS and then are compared with individual state standards. A passing score varies from state to state.

Printed in the United States of America   œ-1

ILTS Assessment of Professional Teaching Tests 101-104 Practice Test 1
ISBN: 978-1-60787-197-2

Assessment of Professional Teaching Tests 101-104 Pre-Test

1. Young children engaging in "parallel" activities are demonstrating their _____ abilities.

    A. Social developmental
    B. Cognitive developmental
    C. Physical developmental
    D. Emotional developmental

2. Mrs. Seville is concerned about a child in her early childhood class. She feels his language is delayed and wants to address this with his parents. What professional quality of an effective teacher is Mrs. Seville demonstrating?

    A. Genuine concern
    B. Knowledge of appropriate learning milestones
    C. Desire for the student to catch up
    D. Understanding of the need for language

3. During which cognitive developmental stage does language develop?

    A. Sensorimotor
    B. Preoperational
    C. Concrete operational
    D. Formal operational

4. Delays in a student's mathematical reasoning would constitute what type of delay?

    A. Physical
    B. Cognitive
    C. Social
    D. Emotional

5. Research pertaining to high expectations in the classroom has revealed:

    A. a direct correlation between teacher expectations and student performance
    B. an indirect correlation between teacher expectations and student performance
    C. a weak correlation between teacher expectations and student performance
    D. that even diluted expectations improve overall student performance

6. Equal opportunity to learn for a student refers to:

    A. each student's right to not be physically impeded from a learning environment
    B. each student's right to be valued the same as other students
    C. each student's right to the same instruction as other students
    D. each student's right that instruction and evaluation are structured to what the student has learned

7. Jenny's teacher has her write her homework in an Agenda book each day, record objectives for her learning centers each day, and journal about her successes each week. Jenny's teacher is targeting the development of:

   A. decision-making skills
   B. goal-setting skills
   C. workplace skills
   D. organizational skills

8. Identifying an issue, listing options/choices, evaluating consequences, and defining ones goals are just some of the strategies designed to:

   A. teach students the appropriate skills to enhance decision-making skills
   B. teach students how to become better organized
   C. increase a teacher's classroom management
   D. All of the above.

9. According to the _____, teachers demonstrate engaging behaviors to students (such as listening with care, demonstrating respect, and enabling positive thinking) which are intended to increase a student's self-concept.

   A. responsive classroom theory
   B. invitational education approach
   C. cooperative learning theory
   D. Constructivist learning theory

10. Recent research indicates that an average child experiences their first risky behavior as early as age:

    A. 8
    B. 10
    C. 12
    D. 14

11. Which of the following statements best describes a teacher's role in encouraging diversity in his or her classroom?

    A. The teacher must ensure all aspects of education are available to all students
    B. The teacher must actively promote inclusion
    C. The teacher must create lesson plans that develop heterogeneous groups
    D. All of the above

12. According to the _____, students learn how different cultures engage in communication so that they understand cultural norms and have a greater perception of integrated global culture.

    A. personalized learning communication model
    B. intercultural communication model
    C. cooperative learning theory
    D. interrelationships theory

13. Differentiating the _____ of a lesson means students who have access to material that interests them.

    A. process
    B. product
    C. subject
    D. content

14. Emergent curriculum refers to:

    A. a teaching strategy that utilizes small groups of students working together.
    B. the development of lessons and projects that are inspired by students' interests.
    C. a learning theory that suggests humans generate knowledge and meaning from their own experiences.
    D. the idea that specialized instruction supports need to be in place to facilitate learning.

15. The main distinction between goals and objectives is that _____ are challenges for the long-term, while _____ are specific and measureable.

    A. objectives.....goals
    B. goals......lessons
    C. goals.....objectives
    D. units......objectives

16. Which of the following is NOT important when considering planning goals and objectives for classroom instruction?

    A. goals and objectives should be significant to the students
    B. goals and objectives must be clear to the teacher, students and any other people in the classroom
    C. goals and objectives must span multiple ages
    D. goals and objectives must be able to be assessed

17. Mr. Parker, a third grade teacher, has consulted his students' records, conducted an informal reading inventory, and interviewed each student about his or her academic interests. These steps indicate that Mr. Parker is attempting to:

    A. gauge student readiness
    B. evaluate his own effectiveness
    C. set students up for a cooperative learning lesson
    D. plan which textbook program to implement

18. Which of the following items would be considered "assistive technology"?

    A. Digital whiteboard
    B. Textbooks with accompanying DVDs and maps
    C. media centers
    D. Speech-to-text software

19. When considering the elements critical to the learning process, _____ describes how student learning will be supported using the learning goals.

    A. learning experiences
    B. lesson content
    C. quality of materials
    D. assessments

20. When is the best time for a teacher to allocate time for students to self-reflect on a lesson's learning objective?

    A. Before a difficult skill is utilized
    B. As independent research is being conducted in groups
    C. After a difficult task is introduced
    D. Before complex materials have been introduced

21. Brain-based learning suggests:

    A. students learn in multiple ways such as spatially or intrapersonally
    B. knowledge about the way the brain retains information enables educators to design the most effective learning environments
    C. students learn optimally when they are given opportunities to construct their own learning.
    D. All of the above

22. Ms. Becker has planned six literacy activities for her second grade language arts block of almost two hours, including activities such as a read aloud, a student pair-share, and a writing center. This morning schedule indicates Ms. Becker:

    A. doesn't think the students can work on a task for any length of time
    B. has a lot of curriculum to cover and is running behind
    C. has a class of students who like to work on language arts
    D. is aware of young students' age-appropriate learning needs

23. What of the following statements is NOT an optimal way for teachers to show they are committed to diverse learning needs and styles in the classroom?

    A. alternate ways in which lessons are taught
    B. provide students with choices for learning
    C. account for individual differences in academic and critical thinking
    D. provide the same assessment to all students

24. A skill which targets how learning in one specific subject area can be applied to other subject areas is considered:

    A. a critical thinking skill
    B. a lower ordered skill
    C. a higher ordered skill
    D. a communication skill

25. When learning how to conduct research in elementary school, students need to identify a list, or _____, of what the project needs and will include.

    A. purpose
    B. visuals
    C. procedure
    D. objective

26. Mrs. Weaver varies her pronunciation, phrasing and rate when teaching her class. These variations indicate that Mrs. Weaver is aware of how variety in _____ is one factor that enhances student learning and attentiveness.

    A. body language
    B. interactive lessons
    C. expression
    D. speech

27. Activities that promote student success in a success-oriented classroom:

    A. allow set amounts of time to learn each skill
    B. provide opportunities for limited feedback and monitoring
    C. allow the students to only work in groups
    D. are based on content that is relevant, clear, and specific

28. Which of the following statements describes the adaptation state of learning?

    A. Teachers stress independent problem-solving and engage in almost no direct instruction
    B. Teachers focus on student feedback and error correction while emphasizing rewards for accuracy
    C. Teachers begin to withdraw direct instruction while emphasizing mnemonic techniques and intrinsic reinforcement
    D. Teachers engage primarily in demonstration and guidance while helping students work through each step of a lesson or project

29. The optimal time to introduce and implement a classroom management plan is:

    A. a few weeks into the semester when the students know the teacher
    B. on multiple occasions over the first days of class
    C. at the "teachable" moment when it is needed
    D. when it is absolutely necessary

30. In order to establish a classroom that displays a teacher's ongoing enthusiasm for learning, teachers must NOT:

    A. drone on about a topic
    B. read during silent reading, alongside the students
    C. use positive non-verbal communication with students
    D. provide interesting personal anecdotes and digressions

31. Mr. Beagly ensures his classroom has ample space, is well-equipped, and arranged in a setup conducive to learning. These considerations demonstrate that Mr. Beagley:

    A. supports an "invitational learning" environment
    B. understands student comfort is a factor or education success
    C. knows the physical setting of the classroom contribute to student learning
    D. All of the above

32. State of furniture and equipment, lighting, and ventilation are all factors concerning the _____ of a classroom.

    A. environment
    B. safety
    C. diversity
    D. atmosphere

33. Which of the following methods is NOT considered a tool in beginning a class quickly and effectively?

    A. turning on an over-head projector
    B. stating the objective and learning activities
    C. having all of the materials prepared, organized per lesson and available
    D. giving instructions to the two students who were absent yesterday

34. Which of the following definitions best describes "group fragmentation"?

    A. breaking students into groups for cooperative learning
    B. moving students in groups and clusters rather than individually
    C. dissolving groups that are not working together well
    D. none of the above

35. **Why do some teachers introduce a lesson, a unit, and/or the school year with ice-breaking activities?**

    A. To fill large amounts of time due to block schedules
    B. For students to become comfortable and familiar with their peers
    C. dissolving groups that are not working together well
    D. none of the above

36. **Which of the following statements is a factor for interpersonal & small-group skills, one of the five elements of cooperative learning?**

    A. groups should periodically self-assess
    B. groups are encouraged to practice leadership, trust-building, and communication
    C. frequent observation of groups helps to monitor participation
    D. students will re-teach concepts as part of their participation

37. **With regards to technology to assist teachers, which statement below does NOT apply?**

    A. School districts are incorporating electronic grading and tracking programs into their curriculums
    B. Federal-mandated standards are not affecting the use of technology in the classroom
    C. Teachers can create web sites and online calendars to create a "communication bridge" between the class and home
    D. Many districts have web applications to collect student data

38. **The role of a _____ in the classroom is to aid the teacher, ensure the class runs smoothly, work with students individually, and continue his or her own education to keep current with educational trends.**

    A. volunteer
    B. student
    C. guest speaker
    D. paraprofessional

39. **This behavior psychologist developed behavior management theories which suggested immediate praise should be offered to students, instantaneous feedback, should be given, and rewards given to encourage proper behavior in the classroom.**

    A. Jean Piaget
    B. B. F. Skinner
    C. Sigmund Freud
    D. Erik Erikson

40. **A _____ is a visual or verbal cue that assists a student through the behavior shaping process?**

    A. contingency
    B. model
    C. token
    D. prompt

41. **Following directions the first time, waiting for permission to talk, staying on task and remaining in one's seat while the teacher is speaking are all common behavior expectations of what grade level?**

    A. Early Childhood classrooms
    B. Young or Lower Elementary classrooms
    C. Upper Elementary or Middle School Classrooms
    D. High School Classrooms

42. **Mrs. Andrews is an energetic teacher who smiles during her lessons and moves around the classroom, eager to help and engage her students. What does this behavior indicate Mrs. Andrews knows about how an effective teacher communicates?**

    A. A teacher's body language has a significant effect on student achievement and learning goals
    B. A teacher's positive learning environment affects student motivation
    C. Angry or blank expressions are perceived by students as a sign of displeasure or disapproval
    D. All of the above

43. **Ben has raised his hand to answer his teacher's question, "What is an example of an herbivore?" Ben is called on and responds, "A bear." Which of the following ways is the best way for her to respond to Ben's incorrect answer?**

    A. "Sorry, Ben. That is wrong."
    B. "Bears eat plants *and* animals, so a bear is a good example of an omnivore, Ben. We need an example of an animal that *only* eats plants."
    C. "Incorrect. Did you hear the description of an herbivore, Ben?"
    D. "Can someone help Ben with the right answer?"

44. **Why is allowing sufficient "wait time" to pass after a teacher-directed question important?**

    A. allows students with some, but not enough, time to process and prepare a response
    B. observe student reactions to the question as a clue to their understanding
    C. to fluster the students
    D. demonstrates that the teacher believes the students do not actually know the answer.

45. **Concepts taught in a(n) _____ manner encourage students to consider simple facts or statements to arrive at more general conclusion?**

    A. cooperative
    B. inductive
    C. deductive
    D. inferential

46. **Which of the following is an effective and appropriate strategy to help students grasp complex ideas while scaffolding students to think critically?**

    A. utilizing visual and tactile aids to help students make connections
    B. present information in large chunks
    C. present new ideas in isolation so as not to be confusing to the student
    D. display information with one sensory approach at a time to keep it simpler

47. **It is vital for teachers to _____ their instructional techniques in order to enhance student learning and retention.**

    A. simplify
    B. accelerate
    C. maintain
    D. vary

48. **According to Bloom's Taxonomy of thinking skills, when students are asked to classify, explain, organize and recall, the students are working on which of the six levels of the cognitive domain?**

    A. synthesis
    B. application
    C. knowledge
    D. understanding

49. **Mrs. Donnelly has noticed that her ninth grade class is lacking in motivation. What strategy could she use to increase the motivation level in her class?**

    A. Ask the students lower-level questions to simplify the material
    B. Ask the students higher-ordered questions to spark curiosity
    C. Ask the students to simply complete the assignments
    D. Ask the students factual recall questions to boost confidence

50. **Which of the following sequences is the correct way for teachers to create a framework of curriculum activities?**

    1. Create a framework of varied instructional learning activities.
    2. Become familiar with what the students are expected to do next year.
    3. Understand abilities of students (taking into account individual differences and special needs).
    4. Become familiar with what the students did last year.

    A. 4, 3, 1, 2
    B. 3, 4, 2, 1
    C. 1, 4, 2, 3
    D. 1, 2, 3, 4

51. **Teachers must make sure that the materials in their classrooms are:**

    A. Accurate and current
    B. Useful
    C. Connected to the curriculum
    D. All of the above

52. **Intrinsic motivation is motivation that comes from:**

    A. within
    B. rewards
    C. teachers
    D. the desire to please

53. **Which of the following is a factor which affects students' motivation in school?**

    A. Basic expectations
    B. Emphasis on grades
    C. Consistent instructional strategies
    D. Assignments given in a timely manner

54. **Which of the following strategies is NOT a suggested way to enhance student motivation in the classroom?**

    A. Planning interactive, hands-on activities
    B. create daily lists and goals
    C. break tasks into large steps
    D. have students identify their connections with the assignment

55. **The hardware of a computer refers to:**

    A. the physical components that make up the computer
    B. the programs that enable the machine to perform jobs
    C. wires that connect the computer to the wall and printers
    D. the network of computers that is linked together

56. Which of the following would be considered the FIRST step in evaluating a software program?

    A. consider the cost of the program
    B. run the program and make deliberate mistakes as a student might
    C. run the program as though you are a student
    D. read the instructions thoroughly to become familiar with the program

57. Mrs. Donaldson notices Barry, a sixth grade student, texting beneath his desk. What is the best course of action for Mrs. Donaldson to take?

    A. instruct Barry to put the phone down
    B. have Barry put the phone is his bag or locker or hold it at her desk until the end of the day
    C. send Barry to the principal
    D. call Barry's parents

58. All of the following are useful applications for technology in the classroom except one. Which is NOT a useful application for students?

    A. access libraries around the world
    B. locate online journals from various sources
    C. create an academic presentation using technology
    D. access social networks

59. There are many steps students can take to evaluate Internet resources for both accuracy and validity. Which of these steps is NOT a step to evaluating Internet resources?

    A. discussing possible popular sites with the class and teacher
    B. analyzing the author's credentials
    C. disregarding the time frame a resource was written
    D. factoring in the audience for which the piece was written

60. When dividing technological tools into primary categories for use in schools, which of the following statements describes the category of research?

    A. instructional or assessment programs that students work on to demonstrate learning
    B. use of worksheets, graphics and other multi-media tools to demonstrate learning
    C. use of the Internet, databases or programs to find new information
    D. All of the above

61. Ms. Andrews' class is working on research presentations using Power Point on the classroom's six computers. Being that there are 19 students in her class, how can Ms. Andrews manage her students so that all get the same opportunity on the classroom computers to complete their work?

    A. rotate individually or in pairs to computer centers
    B. reward the well-behaved students with additional computer time
    C. work on a first-come, first-served basis
    D. allow prepared students to work on the computers as long as they need

62. What is important for teachers to remember when having students collaborate and problem solve using computers together?

    A. all students are proficient so assign work accordingly
    B. if students are good at one technological application, that does not automatically mean they are good at all other applications
    C. technological tools are not that complicated nowadays, so individual work is actually best
    D. social opportunities using technology actually waste the students' time and makes them less effective workers

63. _____refers to the "end result" or format a technologically produced product takes?

    A. Content-delivery
    B. Relevance
    C. Design
    D. Audience

64. When considering equal use of technology in the classroom, teacher need to:

    A. ensure all students have similar opportunities to use technology
    B. realize all students have some technological background
    C. note that students are willing to share their technological weakness with them
    D. realize group work wastes the students' time when working on a computer

65. Which of the following statements is considered a purpose of assessment?

    A. to identify students' strengths and weaknesses
    B. to assess effectiveness of an instructional strategy
    C. to provide data that assists in decision making
    D. All of the above

66. **The fact that some types of assessments are affected by the people involved in administering them is a:**

    A. disadvantage of informal assessments
    B. problem lower-achieving students encounter
    C. disadvantage of formal assessments
    D. disadvantage of objective tests

67. **_____ assessments present students with a real-world task which they must solve by applying the learned knowledge and skills from a prior unit or lesson.**

    A. Subjective
    B. Objective
    C. Informal
    D. Authentic

68. **According to educational researchers, the best way to test the students' ability to organize and present ideas is with the:**

    A. multiple choice item
    B. essay item
    C. true/false item
    D. matching item

69. **When teachers are limited for time and can't provide extensive feedback for every written assignment, what is another alternative on which teachers can rely to help provide students with timely and effective feedback?**

    A. use of writing rubrics
    B. reduce the number of writing assignments
    C. use a spellchecking and grammar checking program to help
    D. All of the above

70. **Ms. Berkley has scored her class's last physics quiz, and she has noted that the majority of students got the same questions incorrect. In the next class, Ms. Berkley reviewed the lesson objectives and quiz questions with the entire class in both the original manner, as well as in an alternative way. The use of this review demonstrates that Ms. Berkley:**

    A. second-guessed her ability to teach the material clearly the first time
    B. knows an effective teacher adjusts lessons to meet the learning needs of her students
    C. was ahead in her lesson plans with time to review
    D. knew her original lesson was not well-planned

71. Why is it important for teachers to begin the year in a way that welcomes open communication between the teacher and the students' home?

    A. It shows the teacher means business from the start of the year
    B. It demonstrates the teacher is friendly
    C. It sets an open and positive tone with families
    D. It shows the teacher is organized

72. Which of the following is NOT an optimal way for teachers to increase parent involvement in school?

    A. Have parents assist with workshops and centers
    B. Organize a small group of room parents for parties and class trips
    C. Invite parents to read with the class
    D. Have parents teach a morning of academic subjects

73. Teachers today are working with an increasingly diverse group of cultures in their classrooms. This requires teachers to establish a positive _____ that suggests their mission is to develop educated and well-rounded students.

    A. curriculum
    B. behavior management system
    C. professional background
    D. tone

74. Mr. Barry has encountered a behavior problem with Sarah, one of his fourth grade students. He is now quite frustrated with her outbursts in class. What is the best way for Mr. Barry to initiate a conversation with Sarah's parents?

    A. wait a few days, cool down, and call them in a professional manner
    B. call the parents immediately while the incident is fresh in his mind
    C. ignore the incident as she is unlikely to improve anyway
    D. call the parents the next day and suggest their daughter is a problem in his class

75. When is the best time for a teacher to collect samples of school work, assessment information, records of behavior, anecdotal records, and other important information for a parent-teacher conference?

    A. prior to the conference
    B. during the conference
    C. after the conference to send them home
    D. it is not necessary to compile this information

76. **Which of the following statements is NOT a way that community involvement can influence and enrich student learning and experiences?**

    A. lecturing in classrooms regarding behavior problems with the students
    B. creating mentoring opportunities
    C. developing paid internships
    D. providing parent-student-community forums to create public voices and discussions

77. **In this type of cooperative teaming, teachers in one grade level work to integrate all of the subjects taught across the grade.**

    A. team
    B. vertical
    C. lateral
    D. horizontal

78. **The role of a district's Child Study Team/Core Team is to:**

    A. work in the regular education classroom with students with special needs
    B. evaluate and provide assistance for students with a variety of needs
    C. execute administrative tasks
    D. lead the development and implementation of a subject area

79. **Which of the following is a reason why mentoring programs for new teachers are an important element in schools?**

    A. new teachers can handle all the work
    B. mentors offer guidance in all areas including curriculum, classroom management, and staff responsibilities
    C. research suggests new teachers succeed with or without mentoring
    D. mentors only offer emotional support to new teachers

80. **Professional development is considered crucial to positive student achievement because:**

    A. it provides opportunities for teacher performance to improve
    B. it enhances instructional practices and techniques
    C. it encourages teachers to provide student-centered learning communities
    D. All of the above

81. Mrs. McAffey has concerns about Brian, one of her first grade students. Brian is demonstrating some anxiety in the classroom as well as trouble with processing directions. She has observed him tapping his desk over and over with his pencil, even after she has implemented some behavioral modification strategies to stop him from doing so. These observations seem to be affecting his class work significantly. What should be Mrs. McAffey's first step to address these concerns?

    A. discuss this with a member of the Child Study Team
    B. discuss this with a colleague
    C. discuss this with her husband
    D. discuss this with the student

82. The _____ refers to the mandate that children be educated to the maximum extent appropriate with their non-disabled peers and specifically to the environment most like that of typical children in which the child with the disability can succeed academically.

    A. Individualized Education Plan
    B. least restrictive environment
    C. concept of mainstreaming
    D. concept of inclusion

83. What is the role of "fair use" with regards to copyright laws?

    A. create a balance between copyright protection and the needs of learners
    B. to enforce copyright laws
    C. to allow copying of any educational materials
    D. to permit copying of videotaping

84. The significance of the 1975 ruling in the media copyright case of Williams & Wilkings Co., v US was that it ruled:

    A. the burden of proving infringement is upon the plaintiff
    B. entire articles may be mass-duplicated for use which advances the public welfare without economic harm to the publisher
    C. in favor of the removal of certain books from school libraries
    D. None of the above

85. Educational research has suggested that one of the greatest obstacles for new teachers is:

    A. steady levels of behavioral issues in the classroom
    B. dealing with students who are minimally involved in the learning process
    C. maintaining a toolkit of fresh instructional strategies
    D. developing a student to his or her full potential

86. **A student's permanent record is:**

    A. a collection of alternative assessments
    B. anecdotal records of classroom performance
    C. a record of attendance and assessments
    D. a file of the student's cumulative educational history

87. **Confidentiality concerning a student's permanent record applies to:**

    A. assessment scores and medical records
    B. every piece of information in the permanent file
    C. personal information only
    D. academic and personal information

88. **The appropriateness, meaningfulness, and usefulness of the inferences from the tests scores refers to the _____ of an assessment.**

    A. reliability
    B. accuracy
    C. validity
    D. cultural significance

89. **Under the US Department of Education, state service centers conduct research in education and:**

    A. run the day-to-day operations of a school
    B. govern school districts
    C. control public education
    D. distribute it to school systems

90. **As a vital member of a school district, the effective teacher must:**

    A. advocate for students
    B. volunteer time and effort
    C. vocalize concerns in a professional manner
    D. All of the above

Assessment of Professional Teaching Tests 101-104 Rationales

1. Young children engaging in "parallel" activities are demonstrating their _____ abilities.

    A. Social developmental
    B. Cognitive developmental
    C. Physical developmental
    D. Emotional developmental

Answer: A. Social developmental.
Part of social development is the awareness of peers. Young children engaging in parallel play are demonstrating a phase of social development where they play alongside another peer, but have a lack of concern for their presence. In other words, they are not playing directly together.

2. **Mrs. Seville is concerned about a child in her early childhood class. She feels his language is delayed and wants to address this with his parents. What professional quality of an effective teacher is Mrs. Seville demonstrating?**

    A. Genuine concern
    B. Knowledge of appropriate learning milestones
    C. Desire for the student to catch up
    D. Understanding of the need for language

Answer: B. Knowledge of appropriate learning milestones.
Teachers should have a broad knowledge and understanding of the phases of development which typically occur in each stage of life, and the teacher must be aware of how receptive children are to specific methods of instruction and learning during each period of development. In this case, Mrs. Seville is aware her student is not meeting language milestones appropriate to his age.

3. During which cognitive developmental stage does language develop?

    A. Sensorimotor
    B. Preoperational
    C. Concrete operational
    D. Formal operational

Answer: B. Preoperational
The preoperational stage refers to children between 18 months to age 7, or toddlerhood through early childhood. It is around 18 months to 2 years of age that the majority of a child's language develops.

4. Delays in a student's mathematical reasoning would constitute what type of delay?

   A. Physical
   B. Cognitive
   C. Social
   D. Emotional

Answer: B. Cognitive
Cognitive delays include verbal and non-verbal domains. In other words, cognitive skills are a student's thinking skills and include skills such as reasoning, verbal skills, memorization, and visual and/or auditory processing.

5. Research pertaining to high expectations in the classroom has revealed:

   A. a direct correlation between teacher expectations and student performance
   B. an indirect correlation between teacher expectations and student performance
   C. a weak correlation between teacher expectations and student performance
   D. that even diluted expectations improve overall student performance

Answer: A. a direct correlation between teacher expectations and student performance.
Part of social development is the awareness of peers. Young children engaging in parallel play are demonstrating a phase of social development where they play alongside another peer, but have a lack of concern for their presence. In other words, they are not playing directly together.

6. Equal opportunity to learn for a student refers to:

   A. each student's right to not be physically impeded from a learning environment
   B. each student's right to be valued the same as other students
   C. each student's right to the same instruction as other students
   D. each student's right that instruction and evaluation are structured to what the student has learned

Answer: C. each student's right to the same instruction as other students
Equal Opportunity to Learn requires that every student have equal access to all resources, physical and intellectual, as well as equal instruction and support from the classroom teacher and staff.

7. **Jenny's teacher has her write her homework in an Agenda book each day, record objectives for her learning centers each day, and journal about her successes each week. Jenny's teacher is targeting the development of:**

   A. decision-making skills
   B. goal-setting skills
   C. workplace skills
   D. organizational skills

Answer: B. goal-setting skills.
By having students write down what they are to accomplish (Agenda book), record and internalize the lesson objectives, and then reflect on how they performed on each task, Jenny's teacher is encouraging the students to reflect on the goals that were set and how she performed in achieving such goals.

8. **Identifying an issue, listing options/choices, evaluating consequences, and defining ones goals are just some of the strategies designed to:**

   A. teach students the appropriate skills to enhance decision-making skills
   B. teach students how to become better organized
   C. increase a teacher's classroom management
   D. All of the above.

Answer: A. teach students the appropriate skills to enhance decision-making skills
When students are given appropriate skills and lessons to learn how to make better decisions, their confidence as an individual and as a student also increase. The items listed in the question are just some of the skills teachers can share with student to help them become better decision-makers.

9. **According to the _____, teachers demonstrate engaging behaviors to students (such as listening with care, demonstrating respect, and enabling positive thinking) which are intended to increase a student's self-concept.**

   A. responsive classroom theory
   B. invitational education approach
   C. cooperative learning theory
   D. Constructivist learning theory

Answer: B. invitational education approach.
According to the invitational education approach, teachers and their behaviors may be inviting or they may be disinviting. Inviting behaviors enhance self-concept among students, while disinviting behaviors diminish self-concept. Inviting teacher behaviors reflect an attitude of "doing with" rather than "doing to."

10. Recent research indicates that an average child experiences their first risky behavior as early as age:

   A. 8
   B. 10
   C. 12
   D. 14

Answer: C. 12
According to the Institute of Youth Development (www.youthdevelopment.org), many children experience their first encounters with drugs, cigarettes, and sexual activity by age 12 (and sometimes even younger).

11. Which of the following statements best describes a teacher's role in encouraging diversity in his or her classroom?

   A. The teacher must ensure all aspects of education are available to all students
   B. The teacher must actively promote inclusion
   C. The teacher must create lesson plans that develop heterogeneous groups
   D. All of the above

Answer: D. All of the above.
Answers A, B, and C are all responsibilities of a teacher. Acceptance of diversity and any specific requirements necessary to aid individuals to accomplish on a par with classmates, must be incorporated in lesson planning, teacher presentation, and classroom activities.

12. According to the _____, students learn how different cultures engage in communication so that they understand cultural norms and have a greater perception of integrated global culture.

   A. personalized learning communication model
   B. intercultural communication model
   C. cooperative learning theory
   D. interrelationships theory

Answer: B. intercultural communication model.
In the intercultural communication model, students are able to learn how different cultures engage in both verbal and nonverbal modes of communicating meaning. Students who understand how to effectively communicate with diverse cultural groups are able to maximize their own learning experiences by being able to transmit both verbally and non-verbally cues and expectations in project collaborations and in performance-based activities.

13. Differentiating the _____ of a lesson means students who have access to material that interests them.

    A. process
    B. product
    C. subject
    D. content

Answer: D. content
The content of a lesson deals with what the teacher will teach, as well as what the teacher wants the students to learn. In a differentiated environment, adjusting the content means that students will have access to content that piques their interest about a topic, with a complexity that provides an appropriate challenge to their intellectual development.

14. Emergent curriculum refers to:

    A. a teaching strategy that utilizes small groups of students working together.
    B. the development of lessons and projects that are inspired by students' interests.
    C. a learning theory that suggests humans generate knowledge and meaning from their own experiences.
    D. the idea that specialized instruction supports need to be in place to facilitate learning.

Answer: B. the development of lessons and projects that are inspired by students' interests.
Emergent curriculum describes the projects and themes that classrooms embark on that have been inspired by the children's interests. As the teacher gets to know the students, s/he listens to what their interests are and creates a curriculum in response to what s/he learns from observations.

15. The main distinction between goals and objectives is that _____ are challenges for the long-term, while _____ are specific and measureable.

    A. objectives…..goals
    B. goals……lessons
    C. goals…..objectives
    D. units……objectives

Answer: C. goals…..objectives
One of the major differences between a goal and an objective is that a goal is long-term and an objective is specific and observable. Once long-range goals have been identified and established, it is important to ensure that all goals and objectives are in conjunction with student ability and needs. Some objectives may be too basic for a higher level student, while others cannot be met with a student's current level of knowledge.

16. Which of the following is NOT important when considering planning goals and objectives for classroom instruction?

    A. goals and objectives should be significant to the students
    B. goals and objectives must be clear to the teacher, students and any other people in the classroom
    C. goals and objectives must span multiple ages
    D. goals and objectives must be able to be assessed

Answer: C. goals and objectives must span multiple ages
Teachers must ensure that all goals and objectives are age-appropriate. This implies that the lessons teachers teach (and therefore the material the students are assessed on) should be appropriate to the developmental levels of the children in their classrooms.

17. Mr. Parker, a third grade teacher, has consulted his students' records, conducted an informal reading inventory, and interviewed each student about his or her academic interests. These steps indicate that Mr. Parker is attempting to:

    A. gauge student readiness
    B. evaluate his own effectiveness
    C. set students up for a cooperative learning lesson
    D. plan which textbook program to implement

Answer: A. gauge student readiness
To determine the abilities of incoming students, it may be helpful to consult their prior academic records. In addition, administering formal and informal tests will provide current readiness levels, and the teacher may assess the readiness of students for a particular level of instruction by having them demonstrate their ability to perform some relevant task. Teachers should also gauge student readiness by simply asking them about their previous knowledge of the subject or task at hand.

18. Which of the following items would be considered "assistive technology"?

    A. Digital whiteboard
    B. Textbooks with accompanying DVDs and maps
    C. media centers
    D. Speech-to-text software

Answer: D. Speech-to-text software
Assistive technology "offers a bridge between a student's needs and his or her abilities. Familiarity with general categories of assistive technology, such as screen readers, speech-to-text software, word prediction tools, book on tape/cd, personal computers or digital assistants for typing and even calculators, gives a teacher the means to ask questions and access resources for students that will enable a student to succeed.

19. When considering the elements critical to the learning process, _____ describes how student learning will be supported using the learning goals.

   A. learning experiences
   B. lesson content
   C. quality of materials
   D. assessments

Answer: A. learning experiences
Learning Experiences for students describes how student learning will be supported using the learning goals. These include: What prior knowledge or experiences will the students bring to the lesson? How will you check and verify that student knowledge? How will you engage all students in the classroom? How will students who have been identified as marginalized in the classroom be engaged in the lesson unit? And more….

20. When is the best time for a teacher to allocate time for students to self-reflect on a lesson's learning objective?

   A. Before a difficult skill is utilized
   B. As independent research is being conducted in groups
   C. After a difficult task is introduced
   D. Before complex materials have been introduced

Answer: C. After a difficult task is introduced
The process of reflection needs to be planned for both during and after learning situations. Reflective thinking refers to the process of analyzing and making judgments about what has happened. It encourages students to continuously evaluate incoming information and be flexible, if appropriate, in their approach to a task. However, it is best for students to reflect after research either with their group or independently; after the material is gathered.

21. Brain-based learning suggests:

A. students learn in multiple ways such as spatially or intrapersonally
B. knowledge about the way the brain retains information enables educators to design the most effective learning environments
C. students learn optimally when they are given opportunities to construct their own learning.
D. All of the above

Answer: B. knowledge about the way the brain retains information enables educators to design the most effective learning environments

Some of the most prominent learning theories in education today include brain-based learning. Supported by recent brain research, brain-based learning suggests that knowledge about the way the brain retains information enables educators to design the most effective learning environments. As a result, researchers have developed twelve principles (listed in Skill 4.1) that relate knowledge about the brain to teaching practices.

22. Ms. Becker has planned six literacy activities for her second grade language arts block of almost two hours, including activities such as a read aloud, a student pair-share, and a writing center. This morning schedule indicates Ms. Becker:

A. doesn't think the students can work on a task for any length of time
B. has a lot of curriculum to cover and is running behind
C. has a class of students who like to work on language arts
D. is aware of young students' age-appropriate learning needs

Answer: D. is aware of young students' age-appropriate learning needs

Teachers who switch things around like this are more likely to keep their students' attention, engage their students more, and have a more behaved classroom. Good teachers know how to capitalize on the need of children to move and change topics. Generally, young children should be changing academic activities every 15-20 minutes.

23. What of the following statements is NOT an optimal way for teachers to show they are committed to diverse learning needs and styles in the classroom?

    A. alternate ways in which lessons are taught
    B. provide students with choices for learning
    C. account for individual differences in academic and critical thinking
    D. provide the same assessment to all students

Answer: D. provide the same assessment to all students
One way teachers can show they are committed to the diverse needs of their students is to alternate both the ways that lessons are taught and how knowledge is assessed. If teachers alternate lessons and assessments, this allows some students to be very successful at an activity, but then exposes other students to that type of thinking.

24. A skill which targets how learning in one specific subject area can be applied to other subject areas is considered:

    A. a critical thinking skill
    B. a lower ordered skill
    C. a higher ordered skill
    D. a communication skill

Answer: A. a critical thinking skill
A critical thinking skill is a skill target that teachers help students develop to sustain learning in specific subject areas that can be applied within other subject areas. To develop a critical-thinking approach to the world, children need to know enough about valid and invalid reasoning to ask questions.

25. When learning how to conduct research in elementary school, students need to identify a list, or _____, of what the project needs and will include.

    A. purpose
    B. visuals
    C. procedure
    D. objective

Answer: C. procedure
Organized folders and a procedural list of what the project or presentation needs to include will create a solid research project for students.

26. Mrs. Weaver varies her pronunciation, phrasing and rate when teaching her class. These variations indicate that Mrs. Weaver is aware of how variety in _____ is one factor that enhances student learning and attentiveness.

    A. body language
    B. interactive lessons
    C. expression
    D. speech

Answer: D. speech
A teacher's voice can really make an impression on students. Teachers' voices have several dimensions—volume, pitch, rate, etc. Other speech factors such as communication of ideas, communication of emotion, distinctness/pronunciation, quality variation and phrasing, correlate with teaching criterion scores. These scores show that "good" teachers ("good" meaning teachers who positively impact and motivate students) use more variety in speech than do "less effective" teachers.

27. **Activities that promote student success in a success-oriented classroom:**

    A. allow set amounts of time to learn each skill
    B. provide opportunities for limited feedback and monitoring
    C. allow the students to only work in groups
    D. are based on content that is relevant, clear, and specific

Answer: D. are based on content that is relevant, clear, and specific
Activities that promote student success are not only based on useful, relevant content that is clearly specified, but also information that is organized for easy learning. Students should be allowed sufficient time to learn the skill and is selected for high rate of success, and have opportunities to work independently, self-monitor, and set goals. Finally, teachers should provide for frequent monitoring and corrective feedback and include collaboration in group activities or peer teaching

28. Which of the following statements describes the adaptation state of learning?

    A. Teachers stress independent problem-solving and engage in almost no direct instruction
    B. Teachers focus on student feedback and error correction while emphasizing rewards for accuracy
    C. Teachers begin to withdraw direct instruction while emphasizing mnemonic techniques and intrinsic reinforcement
    D. Teachers engage primarily in demonstration and guidance while helping students work through each step of a lesson or project

Answer: A. Teachers stress independent problem-solving and engage in almost no direct instruction
Learning progresses in stages from initial acquisition, when the student needs a lot of teacher guidance and instruction to adaptation, when the student can apply what he or she has learned to new situations outside the classroom. Adaptation is the final state and it is in this state that teachers stress independent and problem-solving activities, while practically eliminating direct guidance and instruction.

29. The optimal time to introduce and implement a classroom management plan is:

    A. a few weeks into the semester when the students know the teacher
    B. on multiple occasions over the first days of class
    C. at the "teachable" moment when it is needed
    D. when it is absolutely necessary

Answer: B. on multiple occasions over the first days of class
It is important to realize that the best time to implement organization and classroom discipline is at the beginning of a semester or school year with the entire class – not at a moment of crisis or chaos. This knowledge up front increases student expectations for behavior and emphasizes that classroom management will be maintained.

30. **In order to establish a classroom that displays a teacher's ongoing enthusiasm for learning, teachers must NOT:**

    A. drone on about a topic
    B. read during silent reading, alongside the students
    C. use positive non-verbal communication with students
    D. provide interesting personal anecdotes and digressions

Answer: A. drone on about a topic
Many studies have demonstrated that the enthusiasm of the teacher is infectious. If students feel that the teacher is ambivalent about a task, they will also catch that attitude. Answers B, C, and D are all examples that demonstrate the teacher's interest in her students and love of learning.

31. **Mr. Beagly ensures his classroom has ample space, is well-equipped, and arranged in a setup conducive to learning. These considerations demonstrate that Mr. Beagley:**

    A. supports an "invitational learning" environment
    B. understands student comfort is a factor or education success
    C. knows the physical setting of the classroom contribute to student learning
    D. All of the above

Answer: D. All of the above
The physical setting of the classroom contributes a great deal toward the propensity for students to learn. An adequate, well-built, and well-equipped classroom will invite students to learn. This has been called "invitational learning." A classroom must have adequate physical space so students can conduct themselves comfortably.

32. **State of furniture and equipment, lighting, and ventilation are all factors concerning the _____ of a classroom.**

    A. environment
    B. safety
    C. diversity
    D. atmosphere

Answer: B. safety
In all cases, proper care must be taken to ensure student safety. Furniture and equipment should be situated safely at all times. The teacher has the responsibility to report any items of classroom disrepair to maintenance staff, such as broken windows, poor ventilation and lighting issues.

33. Which of the following methods is NOT considered a tool in beginning a class quickly and effectively?

   A. turning on an over-head projector
   B. stating the objective and learning activities
   C. having all of the materials prepared, organized per lesson and available
   D. giving instructions to the two students who were absent yesterday

Answer: D. giving instructions to the two students who were absent yesterday
Effective teachers have rules that deal with controlled interruptions. When a student returns to class after being absent, the student proceeds to the side counter where extra copies of yesterday's work are located. The student takes the work and sits down to begin today's class work. The student is aware that the teacher will deal with individual instructions during seatwork time when it will not disrupt the class momentum.

34. Which of the following definitions best describes "group fragmentation"?

   A. breaking students into groups for cooperative learning
   B. moving students in groups and clusters rather than individually
   C. dissolving groups that are not working together well
   D. none of the above

Answer: B. moving students in groups and clusters rather than individually
Group fragmentation refers to moving students in groups and clusters rather than one by one. For example, if some students do seat work while other students gather for a reading group, the teacher moves the students in pre-determined groups. Instead of calling the individual names of the reading group, which would be time consuming and laborious, the teacher simply says, "Will the blue reading group please assemble at the reading station. The red and yellow groups will quietly do the vocabulary assignment I am now passing out."

35. Why do some teachers introduce a lesson, a unit, and/or the school year with ice-breaking activities?

    A. To fill large amounts of time due to block schedules
    B. For students to become comfortable and familiar with their peers
    C. dissolving groups that are not working together well
    D. none of the above

Answer: B. moving students in groups and clusters rather than individually
Young children should be developing social skills coincidentally with other life skills and academic skills. Most research predicts that an effective grouping will include an approximately equal mix of girls and boys, with the teacher monitoring and encouraging the participation of all in each aspect of the planned activity. Ice Breakers are a great way to get students to establish common ground between participants, get everyone moving, and create an inviting environment.

36. Which of the following statements is a factor for interpersonal & small-group skills, one of the five elements of cooperative learning?

    A. groups should periodically self-assess
    B. groups are encouraged to practice leadership, trust-building, and communication
    C. frequent observation of groups helps to monitor participation
    D. students will re-teach concepts as part of their participation

Answer: B. groups are encouraged to practice leadership, trust-building, and communication
With regards to interpersonal & small-group skills, cooperative learning encourages students to practice their leadership, trust-building, communication, decision-making and conflict-management skills.

37. **With regards to technology to assist teachers, which statement below does NOT apply?**

    A. School districts are incorporating electronic grading and tracking programs into their curriculums
    B. Federal-mandated standards are not affecting the use of technology in the classroom
    C. Teachers can create web sites and online calendars to create a "communication bridge" between the class and home
    D. Many districts have web applications to collect student data

Answer: B. Federal-mandated standards are not affecting the use of technology in the classroom
Federal-mandated state standards are now causing educators to find a more efficient and successful means of tracking and evaluating student performance. School districts are now incorporating electronic grading and tracking programs into their curriculum. Many of these programs allow teachers to perform basic housekeeping tasks, such as recording assignments, creating homework assignments, and calculating grades more efficiently than the traditional paper-pencil method.

38. **The role of a _____ in the classroom is to aid the teacher, ensure the class runs smoothly, work with students individually, and continue his or her own education to keep current with educational trends.**

    A. volunteer
    B. student
    C. guest speaker
    D. paraprofessional

Answer: D. paraprofessional
A paraprofessional is often brought into a classroom for the benefit of the special needs student. The role of the paraprofessional or any teaching assistant in the classroom must be clearly defined to promote the learning experience for all children and avoid an unnecessary hindrance (or worse, conflict of wills) in the classroom. Paraprofessionals are expected to work in all types of educational settings and fulfill the responsibilities in the question above.

39. **This behavior psychologist developed behavior management theories which suggested immediate praise should be offered to students, instantaneous feedback, should be given, and rewards given to encourage proper behavior in the classroom.**

    A. Jean Piaget
    B. B. F. Skinner
    C. Sigmund Freud
    D. Erik Erikson

Answer: B. B. F. Skinner
One of the more influential behavior management theories is from B.F. Skinner, and his theories have been put into practice in school systems in an assortment of ways. Skinner believed immediate praise should be offered to students, instantaneous feedback, should be given, and rewards given to encourage proper behavior in the classroom.

40. **A _____ is a visual or verbal cue that assists a student through the behavior shaping process?**

    A. contingency
    B. model
    C. token
    D. prompt

Answer: D. prompt
A prompt is a visual or verbal cue that assists the child through the behavior shaping process. In some cases, the teacher may use a physical prompt such as guiding a child's hand. Visual cues include signs or other visual aids. Verbal cues include talking a child through the steps of a task. The gradual removal of the prompt as the child masters the target behavior is called fading.

41. **Following directions the first time, waiting for permission to talk, staying on task and remaining in one's seat while the teacher is speaking are all common behavior expectations of what grade level?**

    A. Early Childhood classrooms
    B. Young or Lower Elementary classrooms
    C. Upper Elementary or Middle School Classrooms
    D. High School Classrooms

Answer: B. Young or Lower Elementary classrooms
Each classroom will have their own set of behavior standards and expectations, and also the resulting consequences as well. Rules should very concrete and simple for the students to follow. At the young elementary level (perhaps Grades 1-4) the expectations listed in the question above are common.

42. **Mrs. Andrews is an energetic teacher who smiles during her lessons and moves around the classroom, eager to help and engage her students. What does this behavior indicate Mrs. Andrews knows about how an effective teacher communicates?**

    A. A teacher's body language has a significant effect on student achievement and learning goals
    B. A teacher's positive learning environment affects student motivation
    C. Angry or blank expressions are perceived by students as a sign of displeasure or disapproval
    D. All of the above

Answer: D. All of the above
A teacher's body language has an even greater effect on student achievement and ability to set and focus on goals. Teacher smiles provide support and give feedback about the teacher's affective state. Studies also show that teacher posture and movement are indicators of the teacher's enthusiasm and energy, which emphatically influence student learning, attitudes, motivation, and focus on goals.

43. **Ben has raised his hand to answer his teacher's question, "What is an example of an herbivore?" Ben is called on and responds, "A bear." Which of the following ways is the best way for her to respond to Ben's incorrect answer?**

    A. "Sorry, Ben. That is wrong."
    B. "Bears eat plants *and* animals, so a bear is a good example of an omnivore, Ben. We need an example of an animal that *only* eats plants."
    C. "Incorrect. Did you hear the description of an herbivore, Ben?"
    D. "Can someone help Ben with the right answer?"

Answer: B. "Bears eat plants *and* animals, so a bear is a good example of an omnivore, Ben. We need an example of an animal that *only* eats plants."
It is risky for students to respond to questions in a classroom. If a student is ridiculed or embarrassed by an incorrect response, the student may shut down and not participate thereafter in classroom discussion. This positive response keeps Ben on a positive train of thought and still provides information to all for learning, even from a "wrong" answer.

44. Why is allowing sufficient "wait time" to pass after a teacher-directed question important?

    A. allows students with some, but not enough, time to process and prepare a response
    B. observe student reactions to the question as a clue to their understanding
    C. to fluster the students
    D. demonstrates that the teacher believes the students do not actually know the answer.

Answer: B. observe student reactions to the question as a clue to their understanding
One part of the questioning process is *wait-time*: the time between the question and either the student response or teacher follow-up. Embedded in wait-time are subtle clues about your judgments of a student's abilities and your expectations of individuals and groups. For example, the more time you allow a student to mull through a question, the more you trust his or her ability to answer that question without getting flustered.

45. Concepts taught in a(n)_____ manner encourage students to consider simple facts or statements to arrive at more general conclusion?

    A. cooperative
    B. inductive
    C. deductive
    D. inferential

Answer: C. deductive
Generally speaking, complex concepts can be taught in two manners: deductively or inductively. In a deductive manner, the teacher gives a definition along with one or two examples and one or two non-examples. As a means of checking understanding, the teacher will ask the students to give additional examples or non-examples and perhaps to repeat the definition.

46. Which of the following is an effective and appropriate strategy to help students grasp complex ideas while scaffolding students to think critically?

    A. utilizing visual and tactile aids to help students make connections
    B. present information in large chunks
    C. present new ideas in isolation so as not to be confusing to the student
    D. display information with one sensory approach at a time to keep it simpler

Answer: A. utilizing visual and tactile aids to help students make connections
Extensive research highlights the fact that new learning occurs when novel information is integrated with that which the learner already knows and by incorporating multi-sensory communication tools, as well as considering multiple intelligences. Strategies to simplify complex ideas include utilizing visual and/or tactile aids to help students make connections, breaking ideas into smaller manageable parts (potentially over several days), and relating new ideas to background knowledge and a central, unifying idea.

47. It is vital for teachers to _____ their instructional techniques in order to enhance student learning and retention.

    A. simplify
    B. accelerate
    C. maintain
    D. vary

Answer: D. vary
It is important for teachers to vary their instructional techniques because experiencing a fact or an idea in several different ways or through multiple senses increases the ability to recall it.

48. According to Bloom's Taxonomy of thinking skills, when students are asked to classify, explain, organize and recall, the students are working on which of the six levels of the cognitive domain?

    A. synthesis
    B. application
    C. knowledge
    D. understanding

Answer: C. knowledge
Knowledge includes tasks such as defining, listing, organizing, recalling and labeling. For example, memorizing definitions or famous quotes, is classified under "knowledge," and this skill is low on the taxonomy of learning and should be worked with early in the sequence of teaching. Today, teachers are encouraged to develop instruction that requires thinking at the higher levels.

49. **Mrs. Donnelly has noticed that her ninth grade class is lacking in motivation. What strategy could she use to increase the motivation level in her class?**

    A. Ask the students lower-level questions to simplify the material
    B. Ask the students higher-ordered questions to spark curiosity
    C. Ask the students to simply complete the assignments
    D. Ask the students factual recall questions to boost confidence

Answer: B. Ask the students higher-ordered questions to spark curiosity
Motivational researchers have found several strategies work to help increase classroom motivation. It is recommended that teachers stimulate student curiosity by asking thought-provoking questions. When there is a gap between what students know and what they want to know, teachers will be able to utilize the natural curiosity which arises as a result of that gap by having students explore this discrepancy.

50. **Which of the following sequences is the correct way for teachers to create a framework of curriculum activities?**

    1. Create a framework of varied instructional learning activities.
    2. Become familiar with what the students are expected to do next year.
    3. Understand abilities of students (taking into account individual differences and special needs).
    4. Become familiar with what the students did last year.

    A. 4, 3, 1, 2
    B. 3, 4, 2, 1
    C. 1, 4, 2, 3
    D. 1, 2, 3, 4

Answer: B. 3, 4, 2, 1
Once the teacher is clear on the general abilities of his or her age group (accounting for individual differences, of course), the teacher should begin by informing herself of what the students did the prior year, and what they are expected to do the following year. Then, the teacher can create a framework within which to work.

51. **Teachers must make sure that the materials in their classrooms are:**

    A. Accurate and current
    B. Useful
    C. Connected to the curriculum
    D. All of the above

Answer: D. All of the above
Teachers are responsible in ensuring that the materials in their classrooms are accurate, current, useful, relevant, readable, usable, and age-appropriate.

52. **Intrinsic motivation is motivation that comes from:**

    A. within
    B. rewards
    C. teachers
    D. the desire to please

Answer: A. within
Intrinsic motivation is motivation that comes from within. For example, while some children only read if given extrinsic rewards (e.g., winning an award for the most pages read), other children read because they enjoy it.

53. **Which of the following is a factor which affects students' motivation in school?**

    A. Basic expectations
    B. Emphasis on grades
    C. Consistent instructional strategies
    D. Assignments given in a timely manner

Answer: D. Assignments given in a timely manner
Assignments are given in a timely manner with respect/consideration for outside commitments like jobs, sports, or other extracurricular activities helps to increase motivation. In addition, setting high expectations, emphasizing learning rather than grades, and varying instructional strategies are also all factors in increasing student motivation.

54. **Which of the following strategies is NOT a suggested way to enhance student motivation in the classroom?**

    A. Planning interactive, hands-on activities
    B. create daily lists and goals
    C. break tasks into large steps
    D. have students identify their connections with the assignment

Answer: C. break tasks into large steps
One strategy to increase motivation is to break larger tasks into smaller, more manageable steps. In higher-ordered learning atmospheres, sometimes the projects can appear too challenging. Sometimes students are overwhelmed and prematurely give up on a project when it is presented as a huge, looming assignment.

55. The hardware of a computer refers to:

   A. the physical components that make up the computer
   B. the programs that enable the machine to perform jobs
   C. wires that connect the computer to the wall and printers
   D. the network of computers that is linked together

Answer: A. the physical components that make up the computer
The computer system can be divided into two main parts—the hardware and the software. Hardware can be defined as all the physical components that make up the machine. This includes the monitor, keyboard, mouse and other pieces such as the printer, scanner, touch pads, joysticks, etc.

56. Which of the following would be considered the FIRST step in evaluating a software program?

   A. consider the cost of the program
   B. run the program and make deliberate mistakes as a student might
   C. run the program as though you are a student
   D. read the instructions thoroughly to become familiar with the program

Answer: D. read the instructions thoroughly to become familiar with the program
When evaluating a software program, first one must read the instructions thoroughly. Once the program is installed and ready to run, the evaluator should first run the program as it would be run by a successful student, without deliberate errors but making use of all the possibilities available to the student. Thirdly, the program should be run making deliberate mistakes to test the handling of errors.

57. Mrs. Donaldson notices Barry, a sixth grade student, texting beneath his desk. What is the best course of action for Mrs. Donaldson to take?

   A. instruct Barry to put the phone down
   B. have Barry put the phone is his bag or locker or hold it at her desk until the end of the day
   C. send Barry to the principal
   D. call Barry's parents

Answer: B. have Barry put the phone is his bag or locker or hold it at her desk until the end of the day
District and school policies are developed to provide a consistent language of expectation for students using school technology with an acceptable use policy. However, beyond computer usage in schools, the use of other electronics like I-pods, Walkmans, and cell phones are prohibited in classrooms. Teachers should actively respond to students who misuse public technology intended to enhance the learning process and access for all students.

58. **All of the following are useful applications for technology in the classroom except one. Which is NOT a useful application for students?**

    A. access libraries around the world
    B. locate online journals from various sources
    C. create an academic presentation using technology
    D. access social networks

Answer: D. access social networks
If the classroom computer has Internet access, students can actually talk to people from other parts of the globe or access libraries and journals from all over the world. Having the school's librarian or technology expert as a guest speaker in a classroom provides another method of sharing and modeling proper presentation preparation using technology. However access to email and social networking sites is not an appropriate use of technology for students during classroom time.

59. **There are many steps students can take to evaluate Internet resources for both accuracy and validity. Which of these steps is NOT a step to evaluating Internet resources?**

    A. discussing possible popular sites with the class and teacher
    B. analyzing the author's credentials
    C. disregarding the time frame a resource was written
    D. factoring in the audience for which the piece was written

Answer: C. disregarding the time frame a resource was written
An important factor to consider regarding an Internet resources IS when it was written. For certain research, time will be sensitive.

60. **When dividing technological tools into primary categories for use in schools, which of the following statements describes the category of research?**

    A. instructional or assessment programs that students work on to demonstrate learning
    B. use of worksheets, graphics and other multi-media tools to demonstrate learning
    C. use of the Internet, databases or programs to find new information
    D. All of the above

Answer: C. use of the Internet, databases or programs to find new information
Under the category of research is where students use the internet, databases, or software programs to find new information. While many students are proficient with the internet, teachers should not assume that students know how to properly research a topic online.

61. **Ms. Andrews' class is working on research presentations using Power Point on the classroom's six computers. Being that there are 19 students in her class, how can Ms. Andrews manage her students so that all get the same opportunity on the classroom computers to complete their work?**

    A. rotate individually or in pairs to computer centers
    B. reward the well-behaved students with additional computer time
    C. work on a first-come, first-served basis
    D. allow prepared students to work on the computers as long as they need

Answer: A. rotate individually or in pairs to computer centers
If the number of computers available for student use is limited, the teacher must take a tip from elementary school teachers who are skilled at managing centers. Students can be rotated singly or in small groups to the computer centers as long as they are well oriented in advance to the task to be accomplished and with the rules to be observed. Rules for using the computer should be emphasized with the whole class prior to individual computer usage in advance and then prominently posted.

62. **What is important for teachers to remember when having students collaborate and problem solve using computers together?**

    A. all students are proficient so assign work accordingly
    B. if students are good at one technological application, that does not automatically mean they are good at all other applications
    C. technological tools are not that complicated nowadays, so individual work is actually best
    D. social opportunities using technology actually waste the students' time and makes them less effective workers

Answer: B. if students are good at one technological application, that does not automatically mean they are good at all other applications
It is important to remember that not ALL students are proficient. Many students actually never learned computer use at home, and some actually do not have the tools at home due to the high costs and therefore have no opportunity to practice. Also, not all technology skills transfer. While one student may navigate the web easily, he or she may not be able to use a word processing program with a similar level of expertise. Finally, social opportunities to learn technology will help students to engage in a more productive, friendly, and help-centered fashion.

63. _____ refers to the "end result" or format a technologically produced product takes?

    A. Content-delivery
    B. Relevance
    C. Design
    D. Audience

Answer: C. Design
Design is the format that the product takes. Teachers can (considering developmental level) expect that students will present information in a way that is organized, clear, and straightforward. With design, non-language elements, such as graphics, pictures, sounds, video, etc., can demonstrate an added element of creativity.

64. **When considering equal use of technology in the classroom, teacher need to:**

    A. ensure all students have similar opportunities to use technology
    B. realize all students have some technological background
    C. note that students are willing to share their technological weakness with them
    D. realize group work wastes the students' time when working on a computer

Answer: A. ensure all students have similar opportunities to use technology
Teachers will need to understand that they have a variety of ability levels in their classrooms. Also, a lack of technological proficiency may actually be an embarrassment to students. In addition, teachers must ensure all students have similar opportunities to use technology, particularly as the students with the least home exposure will need more time.

65. **Which of the following statements is considered a purpose of assessment?**

    A. to identify students' strengths and weaknesses
    B. to assess effectiveness of an instructional strategy
    C. to provide data that assists in decision making
    D. All of the above

Answer: D. All of the above
Assessment is observing an event and making a judgment about its status of success. There are seven purposes of assessment, and three of them are listed in Answers A, B, and C. The other four purposes are to assist student learning; to asses and improve the effectiveness of curriculum programs; to assess and improve teacher effectiveness; to communicate with and involve parents.

66. **The fact that some types of assessments are affected by the people involved in administering them is a:**

    A. disadvantage of informal assessments
    B. problem lower-achieving students encounter
    C. disadvantage of formal assessments
    D. disadvantage of objective tests

Answer: A. disadvantage of informal assessments
Informal assessments do provide a picture of abilities across different formats; however informal assessments may not measure specific retention and achievement. Informal assessments tend to be subjective and therefore are affected by the people involved. For example, if the teacher misses something in an observation or is in a bad mood when grading an essay, this may affect the outcome of the assessment.

67. **_____ assessments present students with a real-world task which they must solve by applying the learned knowledge and skills from a prior unit or lesson.**

    A. Subjective
    B. Objective
    C. Informal
    D. Authentic

Answer: D. Authentic
Authentic assessments are a type of assessment that presents students with a real-world task which they must solve by applying their knowledge and skills. Students are typically provided with a rubric or structured outline of how they will be graded. Rubrics tend to focus on performance, skills, and demonstration of knowledge, not just if a student can select a correct answer from four choices.

68. **According to educational researchers, the best way to test the students' ability to organize and present ideas is with the:**

    A. multiple choice item
    B. essay item
    C. true/false item
    D. matching item

Answer: B. essay item
The best way to test the student's ability to organize and present ideas is with the essay test item. This type of test item also utilizes the student's ability to think and problem solve. However, the main drawbacks to this type of question are the unreliability of scoring and the amount of time necessary to score the item.

69. When teachers are limited for time and can't provide extensive feedback for every written assignment, what is another alternative on which teachers can rely to help provide students with timely and effective feedback?

    A. use of writing rubrics
    B. reduce the number of writing assignments
    C. use a spellchecking and grammar checking program to help
    D. All of the above

Answer: A. use of writing rubrics
Although detailed and timely feedback is important—and necessary—teachers do not have to provide it all the time to increase student learning. They can also teach students how to use scoring guides and rubrics to evaluate their own work, particularly before they turn it in. One particularly effective way of doing this is by having students examine models and samples of proficient work.

70. Ms. Berkley has scored her class's last physics quiz, and she has noted that the majority of students got the same questions incorrect. In the next class, Ms. Berkley reviewed the lesson objectives and quiz questions with the entire class in both the original manner, as well as in an alternative way. The use of this review demonstrates that Ms. Berkley:

    A. second-guessed her ability to teach the material clearly the first time
    B. knows an effective teacher adjusts lessons to meet the learning needs of her students
    C. was ahead in her lesson plans with time to review
    D. knew her original lesson was not well-planned

Answer: B. an effective teacher adjusts lessons to meet the learning needs of her students
These examples demonstrate how an expert teacher adjusts lessons to meet the learning needs of students on an on-going basis. It proves that any well-planned lesson still may need adjustment. It also shows that the good teacher should look out for ways to make a good lesson better—even if it's in the middle of the lesson delivery!

71. **Why is it important for teachers to begin the year in a way that welcomes open communication between the teacher and the students' home?**

    A. It shows the teacher means business from the start of the year
    B. It demonstrates the teacher is friendly
    C. It sets an open and positive tone with families
    D. It shows the teacher is organized

Answer: C. It sets an open and positive tone with families
Many elementary teachers choose to start off the year with a friendly letter welcoming the students to her classroom, in addition to introducing herself to the students and their families. In the higher grades, teachers typically provide at least a handout with their course content and contact information as a reference for parents and students. This communication sets an open and positive tone with the families so they know how to reach the teacher and that she is willing to communicate.

72. **Which of the following is NOT an optimal way for teachers to increase parent involvement in school?**

    A. Have parents assist with workshops and centers
    B. Organize a small group of room parents for parties and class trips
    C. Invite parents to read with the class
    D. Have parents teach a morning of academic subjects

Answer: D. Have parents teach a morning of academic subjects
Many teachers devise clever strategies to increase parental involvement at school. Parents are invited in to assist with workshops, attend class trips, participate as a room parents, organize special events, read to the class, speak of an occupation, help with classroom housekeeping, and more. Parents can also be involved by volunteering for the PTO/A, library help, office help, and other tasks. Some teachers plan a few events a year in the classroom for special parties, presentations and events.

73. Teachers today are working with an increasingly diverse group of cultures in their classrooms. This requires teachers to establish a positive _____ that suggests their mission is to develop educated and well-rounded students.

   A. curriculum
   B. behavior management system
   C. professional background
   D. tone

Answer: D. tone
Teachers must show respect to all parents and families. They need to set the tone that suggests that their mission is to develop students into the best people they can be. And then they need to realize that various cultures have different views of how children should be educated.

74. Mr. Barry has encountered a behavior problem with Sarah, one of his fourth grade students. He is now quite frustrated with her outbursts in class. What is the best way for Mr. Barry to initiate a conversation with Sarah's parents?

   A. wait a few days, cool down, and call them in a professional manner
   B. call the parents immediately while the incident is fresh in his mind
   C. ignore the incident as she is unlikely to improve anyway
   D. call the parents the next day and suggest their daughter is a problem in his class

Answer: A. wait a few days, cool down, and call them in a professional manner
When you find it necessary to communicate (whether by phone, letter, or in person) with a parent regarding a concern about a student, allow yourself a "cooling off" period before making contact with the parent. It is important that you remain professional and objective. Your purpose for contacting the parent is to elicit support and additional information that may have a bearing on the student's behavior or performance.

75. **When is the best time for a teacher to collect samples of school work, assessment information, records of behavior, anecdotal records, and other important information for a parent-teacher conference?**

    A. prior to the conference
    B. during the conference
    C. after the conference to send them home
    D. it is not necessary to compile this information

Answer: A. prior to the conference
When a conference is scheduled, whether at the request of the teacher or parent, the teacher should allow sufficient time to prepare thoroughly. Collect all relevant information prior to the conference in order to be prepared. It is also a good idea to compile a list of questions or concerns you wish to address.

76. **Which of the following statements is NOT a way that community involvement can influence and enrich student learning and experiences?**

    A. lecturing in classrooms regarding behavior problems with the students
    B. creating mentoring opportunities
    C. developing paid internships
    D. providing parent-student-community forums to create public voices and discussions

Answer: A. prior to the conference
Both professionally and personally, communities can enrich the student learning experiences by including the strategies in Answers B, C, and D. If a community member chooses to participate in the classroom, it should be for positive purposes such as to ask teachers and students what's needed to promote academic progress and growth.

77. **In this type of cooperative teaming, teachers in one grade level work to integrate all of the subjects taught across the grade.**

    A. team
    B. vertical
    C. lateral
    D. horizontal

Answer: D. horizontal
When in horizontal teams, teachers in one grade level work to integrate all of the subjects taught across the grade. For example, in a team of four fifth grade teachers, teachers may collaborate to find the connections between Language Arts, Science, Math and Social Studies to present interdisciplinary instruction across the entire fifth grade level. This systems cuts down on planning for each teacher and encourages solid educational connections between subjects and material, therefore enhancing the real-life applications of the material, as well as student interest.

78. **The role of a district's Child Study Team/Core Team is to:**

    A. work in the regular education classroom with students with special needs
    B. evaluate and provide assistance for students with a variety of needs
    C. execute administrative tasks
    D. lead the development and implementation of a subject area

Answer: B. evaluate and provide assistance for students with a variety of needs
Many schools have Child Study Teams made up of additional professionals who aid students with various needs. These often include the students' teachers, parents and the inclusion of necessary professionals which could include occupational therapists, special education teachers, speech therapists, guidance counselors, and school psychologists.

79. **Which of the following is a reason why mentoring programs for new teachers are an important element in schools?**

    A. new teachers can handle all the work
    B. mentors offer guidance in all areas including curriculum, classroom management, and staff responsibilities
    C. research suggests new teachers succeed with or without mentoring
    D. mentors only offer emotional support to new teachers

Answer: B. mentors offer guidance in all areas including curriculum, classroom management, and staff responsibilities
New teachers tend to be overwhelmed with the start of their first few school years, and mentors can offer guidance in all areas including classroom setup, materials, organization, classroom management, curriculum implementation, planning, events such as Back To School Night, staff responsibilities, and emotional support. Research supports that implementing strong and effective mentoring programs benefits the new teachers, as well as the student achievement in the new teacher's classroom.

80. **Professional development is considered crucial to positive student achievement because:**

    A. it provides opportunities for teacher performance to improve
    B. it enhances instructional practices and techniques
    C. it encourages teachers to provide student-centered learning communities
    D. All of the above

Answer: D. All of the above
Professional development opportunities for teacher performance improvement or enhancement in instructional practices are essential for creating comprehensive learning communities. The development of student-centered learning communities that foster the academic capacities and learning synthesis for all students should be the fundamental goal of professional development for teachers.

81. Mrs. McAffey has concerns about Brian, one of her first grade students. Brian is demonstrating some anxiety in the classroom as well as trouble with processing directions. She has observed him tapping his desk over and over with his pencil, even after she has implemented some behavioral modification strategies to stop him from doing so. These observations seem to be affecting his class work significantly. What should be Mrs. McAffey's first step to address these concerns?

    A. discuss this with a member of the Child Study Team
    B. discuss this with a colleague
    C. discuss this with her husband
    D. discuss this with the student

Answer: A. discuss this with a member of the Child Study Team
The teacher should take this information to the appropriate committee for discussion and consideration. The committee will recommend the next step to be taken. Often subsequent steps could include a parent interview, a psychological evaluation, and/or physical examinations such as vision and hearing screening and a complete medical examination by a doctor.

82. The _____ refers to the mandate that children be educated to the maximum extent appropriate with their non-disabled peers and specifically to the environment most like that of typical children in which the child with the disability can succeed academically.

    A. Individualized Education Plan
    B. least restrictive environment
    C. concept of mainstreaming
    D. concept of inclusion

Answer: B. least restrictive environment
This is the definition of least restrictive environment. Inclusion, mainstreaming and least restrictive environment are interrelated policies under the IDEA, with varying degrees of statutory imperatives. Mainstreaming is a policy where disabled students can be placed in the regular classroom, as long as such placement does not interfere with the student's educational plan. Inclusion is the right of students with disabilities to be placed in the regular classroom.

83. What is the role of "fair use" with regards to copyright laws?

    A. create a balance between copyright protection and the needs of learners
    B. to enforce copyright laws
    C. to allow copying of any educational materials
    D. to permit copying of videotaping

Answer: B. least restrictive environment
Fair use, especially important to educators, is meant to create a balance between copyright protection and the needs of learners for access to protected material. Fair use is judged by the purpose of the use, the nature of the work (whether creative or informational), the quantity of the work for use, and the market effect. In essence, if a portion of a work is used to benefit the learner with no intent to deprive the author of his profits, fair use is granted.

84. **The significance of the 1975 ruling in the media copyright case of Williams & Wilkings Co., v US was that it ruled:**

    A. the burden of proving infringement is upon the plaintiff
    B. entire articles may be mass-duplicated for use which advances the public welfare without economic harm to the publisher
    C. in favor of the removal of certain books from school libraries
    D. None of the above

Answer: B. entire articles may be mass-duplicated for use which advances the public welfare without economic harm to the publisher
This ruling provides encouragement to educators that fair use may be interpreted more liberally.

85. **Educational research has suggested that one of the greatest obstacles for new teachers is:**

    A. steady levels of behavioral issues in the classroom
    B. dealing with students who are minimally involved in the learning process
    C. maintaining a toolkit of fresh instructional strategies
    D. developing a student to his or her full potential

Answer: B. dealing with students who are minimally involved in the learning process Researchers have shown that for new teachers entering the profession, the two greatest obstacles are dealing with increasing behavioral issues in the classroom and dealing with student minimally engaged in their own learning process. The goal of teachers is to maintain a toolkit of resources to deal with an ever-changing landscape of learners and classroom environments.

86. A student's permanent record is:

    A. a collection of alternative assessments
    B. anecdotal records of classroom performance
    C. a record of attendance and assessments
    D. a file of the student's cumulative educational history

Answer: D. a file of the student's cumulative educational history
The student permanent record is a file of the student's cumulative educational history. It contains a profile of the student's academic background as well as the student's behavioral and medical background. The purpose of the permanent record is to provide applicable information about the student so that the student's individual educational needs can be met.

87. Confidentiality concerning a student's permanent record applies to:

    A. assessment scores and medical records
    B. every piece of information in the permanent file
    C. personal information only
    D. academic and personal information

Answer: B. every piece of information in the permanent file
The most essential fact to remember in regard to students' records is that the information within is confidential. Although specific policies may vary from one school or district to another, confidentiality remains constant and universal.

88. The appropriateness, meaningfulness, and usefulness of the inferences from the tests scores refers to the _____ of an assessment.

    A. reliability
    B. accuracy
    C. validity
    D. cultural significance

Answer: C. validity
Validity refers to the appropriateness, meaningfulness and usefulness of the specific inferences made from test scores. Test validation is the process of accumulating evidence to support such inferences. This means that in order for a test to be valid, the content needs to match the instructional objective and the scores need to support the external criterion (e.g., statewide assessments).

89. **Under the US Department of Education, state service centers conduct research in education and:**

    A. run the day-to-day operations of a school
    B. govern school districts
    C. control public education
    D. distribute it to school systems

Answer: D. distribute it to school systems
Under the US Department of Education are various research and "service" centers. Scattered around the country, these centers conduct research in education and distribute it to school systems around the country. Under the state are local service centers. Usually, these are operated by counties. These service centers provide professional development to teachers and administrators, provide additional student services, and set instructional tones for all districts within the region.

90. **As a vital member of a school district, the effective teacher must:**

    A. advocate for students
    B. volunteer time and effort
    C. vocalize concerns in a professional manner
    D. All of the above

Answer: D. All of the above
As an individual who spends a great deal of time with his or her students, the teacher is one who truly understands what students and schools need. It is important for teachers to vocalize concerns, issue and/or problems regarding their students, class, school and district.

Answer Key

1.	A		31.	D		61.	A
2.	B		32.	B		62.	B
3.	B		33.	D		63.	C
4.	B		34.	B		64.	A
5.	A		35.	B		65.	D
6.	C		36.	B		66.	A
7.	B		37.	B		67.	D
8.	A		38.	D		68.	B
9.	B		39.	B		69.	A
10.	C		40.	D		70.	B
11.	D		41.	B		71.	C
12.	B		42.	D		72.	D
13.	D		43.	B		73.	D
14.	B		44.	B		74.	A
15.	C		45.	C		75.	A
16.	C		46.	A		76.	A
17.	A		47.	D		77.	D
18.	D		48.	C		78.	B
19.	A		49.	B		79.	B
20.	C		50.	B		80.	D
21.	B		51.	D		81.	A
22.	D		52.	A		82.	B
23.	D		53.	D		83.	B
24.	A		54.	C		84.	B
25.	C		55.	A		85.	B
26.	D		56.	D		86.	D
27.	D		57.	B		87.	B
28.	A		58.	D		88.	C
29.	B		59.	C		89.	D
30.	A		60.	C		90.	D

www.ingramcontent.com/pod-product-compliance
Lightning Source LLC
LaVergne TN
LVHW061317060426
835507LV00019B/2189